This page is left deliberately blank except for this sentence which gets in the way of confusing the reader because the page is no longer blank but we can't tell you that and still leave the page blank.

Postage Due

Deep from the depths of the '60s

'60s poetry written on the side of the road, on kitchen
tables in various hovels and along thousands of miles of
coffee shops.

By Bruce Rout

Published by Bruce Rout

ISBN: 978-0-9812096-0-9

Fourth Printing: 2009

This is for Roxy.

How to Read Poetry

When I began the journey into the land of poetry I had always felt that the poet was trying to hide something from me. Perhaps it was so that I would hunt for it and thereby value discovered treasures in the poem even more. Sometimes there is an air of the ironic or subtle in what is trying to be conveyed, I guess. I usually got these feelings as a result of trying to figure out, and write, assignments on poems for high school. Many people read my poems and say they enjoy them but simply haven't a clue what they mean. I honestly didn't try to make things confusing; I guess they just ended up that way. Then, during various readings I would introduce the poem being read and the introduction helped the audience understand, through the poem's setting, what the poem was about. It then became obvious that the audience actually enjoyed the poem more when they understood what it was about. Surprise, surprise.

Then Roxy began reading and trying to understand what I was saying in my poetry. When she finally grasped something of what I was trying to say she would exclaim, "Oh, so that's what it's about! That's much better!" This is somewhat similar to the exclamations of my audiences. It takes a little while for me to get the message, but it does come through eventually. The reader enjoys the poem more when there is some understanding of the poem's setting. OK, I got it.

Now, you can read my poetry any way or any where you like. You can read it in a coffee shop, at home, while driving your car or in the middle of a global thermonuclear war. It doesn't matter. Some of it you may enjoy, and some of it you may not and some may make you react in anger. Good. But there is no need to reach for your high school poetry notes in order to enjoy what I have written. As a matter of fact, if you do reach for your high school poetry notes when reading my poetry, I would be a bit worried. Sometimes there are meanings and sometimes there is a deliberate establishment of cognitive dissonance in the mind of the reader. Sometimes it just sounds nice. Don't read too much into it. The confusion may be deliberate so that a greater insight to knowledge or understanding can be experienced. It's kind of like poetic surgery whereby your chest is opened up so the magic wand of nausea can touch your heart. You get the idea.

Enjoy it. Just read for the sake of reading. The poet's job is to inspire you to think and to feel -- to go to new places. Poetry forms the basis of philosophy which forms the basis of mathematics which forms the basis of physics and establishes for us, our world view. Until of course, it all comes crashing down, like now, and we have to start building it up all over again.

I would like to leave you with the following quotation from John Keats, who died at 26 years of age -- just a kid. It helps to clarify.

'Beauty is truth, truth beauty,—that is all
Ye know on earth, and all ye need to know.'

- John Keats

Table of Contents

Setting to Trilogy ...

Back in the sixties, millions of kids got kicked out of
their homes by their parents and, not having anywhere
to go, began hitch hiking all over North America,
Europe and eventually the world at large. We, as those
who experienced this rejection by their parents, never
really understood why our parents did this. We in turn
have tried to be better parents to our kids than what
our parents were to us. We sincerely hope that our
children will be much better parents than we were.

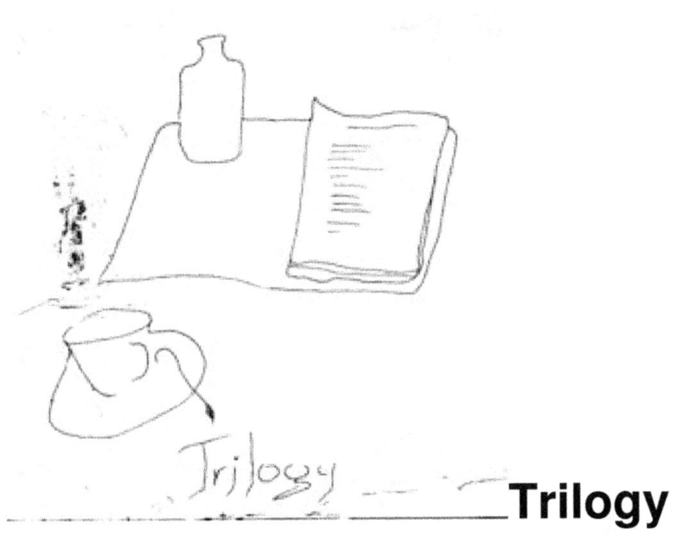

Trilogy

Three poems
written in the 60s
by Bruce Rout

You are alone hundreds and hundreds of miles from
anywhere – from any human habitation or human
being or even piece of litter. You are alone trying to
hitch a ride to anywhere on the Trans Canada
Highway. If you died, no one would know or even care.
Your body would eventually decay and become dirt.
The earth itself, the land, was all that would accept
you. Its arms were always open, waiting for us.

A Weird Poem

I have found a place to live
In the imprint of a northern lake.
And I have stood on the shores
Of a thousand miles of highway.
I have waited for an eternity
In the arms of a wilderness
For you to come and join me
Till your soul leaves its shell
And your body becomes
The land you love.

While walking through a downtown park in Toronto, I noticed a statue of John A. Macdonald, stopped and read the inscription there. The statue was dirty from the birds during the summer in the park. The rest is history.

Poem of National Prejudice

There's the statue of John A.
His head worn bald
By the scratchings of birds' feet
And the gentle massaging of their white and talcum
excretion
Which comes only from the mouth
Of the American Eagle.
It brings the comforting thought
That once a handshake
Froze the complacent minds of men
Into a burning awareness.

But alas, it's only a statue
Standing in a lonely park
Filled with people.
He stands and watches a nation grow
Under the talc of the American eagle.

A Dirty Poem is just that ... a dirty poem. I wrote this while sitting in an all night coffee shop in Edmonton. I ran home to my hitch hiking buddy Bruce Miller and in a fit of excitement woke him up to read it to him. There was a chair there with crap and dirty clothes on it so I sat on the back of the chair and read the poem to him with great exuberance. Miller was amazed and said I had to always read the poem while sitting on the back of a chair. I have complied so far. Bruce and I had many adventures together and after many years of separation I received a letter from his father telling me that he had died in a hunting accident in 1993. But it doesn't take away from the good times we had together as friends trying to find God knows what on the road.

A Dirty Poem

Entree la banque de Montreal
And please wipe your feet.
Quand vous sortez
Watch your step.
For the boogie man awaits you
Just around the corner
Wearing buffalo hide
Blocking the street,
Like plastic maple leaves
That guaranty trust or something.
There's a drunk lying in the street
That everyone ignores
Or there's a fight on Jasper and seventh.
Cops beat people in Montreal
And Marvelous Milvain smokes pot.
Then again there's Dief,
Saying we're approaching
A new horizon,
A new beginning, as he climbs a hill.
But old John's gone
Smothered by an Ottawa fog.
He seems content just to walk
Prairie pipelines in the dark,
Or drawing pictures of flags in the sand.
Bippy hippies running from tearless wonder
And carrying huge flags
With bold red stripes on either end,
A red footprint of a dinosaur in the middle
Framing a picture of Dief
All on a white background.
Red and white, black and yellow,
Green and orange, blue and brown.
See the cows on the farm.
How I wish one'd go down

And meet my lovely at the dell,
Which reminds me of the word hell
And I realize that insanity
Is the inaneness of life's ending glory
Or man's desire to escape
An unknown reality,
Buried deep in the depths of thought.
But stay for a bit
And let me bite your tit
Or play the role as a college grad.
To hell with it I'm sad … or something.
Don't bug me or let me keep myself.
For I'll die another death
A thousand times
And never see an embrace of life
Or kiss of darkness within
A lake's murky bottom
Where lingers rotten tree stumps.
Mud and water trees and sand,
Don't you think that life is grand?
An Indian is here and gone tomorrow.
He'll die at 20,
Which keeps the Eskimo voting population down.
10 Downing Street, April 27, 1921
Where were you then?
In Tiffany's or Paris
Wearing an evening gown?
Or going down to H. M. Dockyards
At dawn to sit by the Thames
And cry or weep
Just like good old T.S.?
Isn't the U.S. a mess?
So long as we don't digress.
We're 10 years ahead of them
And look where they're going.
Pierre Elliott's no fool you know.

Got a degree from U. de M.
Just yesterday I say and cannot come outside
'Cause some broad named Michelle
Is after his body
And he only knows how to kiss
'Cause he's from the East, man!
What's a girl with long hair
And frilly blouse doing here; dear?
Let's swim the river love, on the high 49th.
54-40, 1791, 1867.
Keep it up Quebec
You'll make it yet
And show the world a thing or two.
Sure Levesque sure.
Someone cleaned the bird shit
From John A's head in T.0.
But can't seem to keep him clean
Put a roof over his head, clod.
Even keep him from the sun.
A girl blows bubbles
Floating from Victoria.
We're marching to Pretoria
In rain and sleet.
Rain and sleet, snow and hail
Sunny days are here again
But go at nights end
Tomorrow.
Hollow men walk streets at night
In shadows between decisions
Writing on walls graffiti's revenge
T.S. Elliot was here
And shit everywhere.
Exlax is a form of candy.
Drink Beresford's Beuodenal Balm
And it'll clean your insides
Like porridge never could.

Cities

60s Poetry

**by
Bruce
Rout**

A poem about Toronto to remind me why I left. Toronto
people are good people but the times just weren't right.

Toronto

There is a wall
Which runs from Oshawa
To Hamilton
Via Barrie.

If you ooze under it
And ask any housewife
Shopping with curlers in her hair,
And ask a newspaper
Lying in the street,
And touch any building
From Queen and Young
To Pape and Broadview via Highway 27;
You can smell anywhere you go
A mind is drowned,
That somewhere a guy is mugged,
A girl is being raped,
And a city is dying.

- Bruce Rout

Have you ever been in a riot? I mean, right smack dab in the middle of one? I have – many times and I never wanted nor intended to be there. It is very scary. Guns are going off, people smashing and burning things. It's late and very dark. You're right downtown with no escape and you realize you're the wrong colour. All you can do is tip toe quietly out, avoiding people and not pissing anyone off until you reach some highway miles out of town from where you can hitch hike to safety, probably to the next city where, of course, there is another riot. After this place, I ended up in Chicago with a lot of very crazy people. But that is another story.

View from the Top

I walk the streets alone tonight
And see stripes of pavement
Run red with blood below the stars above,
The glow of streetlights gives a shade of whiteness
And I feel like I'm walking all over
The American flag.
A Negro boy tried to sell me a diamond ring
For fifty cents,
A guy at a meter offered me a quarter for a dime;
These poor people,
All they have are their leaders.
Beneath the flag a Yank stands alone
And waits for his followers to rejoin him,
And as I walk the streets at night—
I know how he feels
And my heart bleeds for him.

- Bruce Rout
Detroit
May 28, 1968

This is one of my favorite poems. I am not going to explain it to you. Just enjoy it.

Edmonton

Canada Dry in iron cement
Wrought by the hand of Sophocles
Has pierced its head
Through the North Saskatchewan
And sang a green, green song:
Flow on sweet river of misery
With your dust soot laden shore
You are walking on the man of love
And have ceased to clean a city
Of white linnen.
Roll over one in tumbling motion
And kick your sides
Like a baby's crib
And sweep the floor
Of war and poverty.

Edmonton O Edmonton...
Your tears flow down
Like peanut butter,
Your streets are dirtied
By clean bare feet,
And your door is closed forever.

'Though I've lain
Between two pine trees
And crawled
Between two blades of wheat
And knelt
Between two mountainous caverns
And stood
With each foot in a different ocean
I've called myself a man –
And wept.

"Leave it in!"
She said to the boy
Who lay in his innocence.
His charm withdrawn
Like a dying magnet
And his arms stripped bare of birch bark.

I've walked night streets
And felt the hand of Christ
Upon my shoulder.
I 've turned
And seen his face to mine,
I've run
I've hidden
I've tried to turn
And walk away,
I've tried to reform
Or be reborn
I've tried to decide
I've tried to be myself
I've tried to be Him
I've tried to die
I've lived
I've tried all forms
Of ointments and treatments
Of burns, of Band-Aid strips,
Of cotton batten.
Bastard child of Mary,
What do you want with me?

Hollow eyes I walk in
Run tears of a surfer's paradise.
Martyrs' wounds
And bloody toenails
Have cursed you
Trying to escape your hold.

Let go damn it
Leave me be
By letting me die
Or at least give me
The peace of mind of wisdom.
Dear God, sweet God,
Whose serpent Satan lies
Around your finger like a ring,
Play your harp for me –
And sing the melody
To wash Hamlet's father
From my mind.

- Bruce Rout
Edmonton, 1968

There were four of us in a '53 flat-head Ford trying to drive from Edmonton to Montreal by way of Los Angeles. There was no where to park in this city – no where. I was exhausted from driving and had to park by a fire hydrant. We got towed. We were in the worst part of town. Miller dragged us all into this dark and barely lit basement filled with black brothers and sisters in the middle of a time of high racial tension. We were scared. There were very dim candles interspersed and a flood light on an old broken guitar at the far back of the room. We got sat next to it. Coming down an improvised aisle came two old black men. One was blind with dark glasses and was carrying a white cane and large harmonica wrapped up in masking tape with a microphone lead dangling from it. He was escorted by, what was obviously, his concerned friend who guided him gently and with trepidation forward towards a ramshackle makeshift stage by where we sat. Miller was ecstatic. He kept hitting me.

"Do you know who that is?" he shouted quietly, "Do you know who that is!!!??"

"No Bruce, I don't know who that is," I replied.

"That's Sonny Brown and Terry McGee!" He screamed almost silently not to disturb the air of sacredness.

The room filled immediately with love, and a sea of smiling black faces in this San Francisco basement taught four naïve white kids the true meaning of the blues for hours and hours through the night

Chocolate Cages

A block of wood
Crushed from either side
Spurts upwards
Like an overcrowded city –
And one more dimension
Is added for man
To understand.

Each groove in wood
Like streets on a city map
Stand as the maze
Each rat must run
Before his daily life is through,
And his reward is granted
By his stops and starts at streetlights.

Give me, oh great and wise
Single pair of dice
The eternal bliss I seek
To have my reward
Of milk and honey
At each light of red and green,
And before my treadmill stops
From lack of inspiration
-- and love.

- Bruce Rout
San Francisco.
Oct. 69

Another blank page that isn't blank.

Women

A series of love poems

written   in the 60s

by

Bruce Rout

Wawa ... what can anyone say about Wawa? It is a very small town hundreds and hundreds of miles from anywhere in the northern Canadian wilderness. The trans Canada Highway runs through it. There are miles and miles of hitch hikers trying to get a lift out of the town going one way and miles and miles of hitch hikers trying to get out of town going the other. There is the story, probably true, of one young man who would hitch hike during the day and drink coffee at the 24-hour Husky gas station to stay warm at night. Eventually he ran out of money and worked washing dishes between shifts trying to hitch hike out of town. He was there for so long he ended up marrying the daughter of the owner of the gas station and may still be there today. His spirit lives on watching over a large statue of a Canada goose.

The Wawa Poems

A series
of poems
about my
first marriage
and subsequent
divorce.

After Seeing Lake Superior Just West of Wawa

I dream of Margaret
When I stare at a candle.
I can see her eyes
In the heart of light.
I can see her lips
On the flicker of a flame,
And I can see her delicacy
Enclosed in a slender wick.
She pierces my memory
In the background of my thought.
If I touch her she will extinguish
And if I go away I will die.

Dec. 10/ 68

- Bruce Rout
Waterloo

West of Wawa

I don't know how to tell you when I'm blind
I don't know how to say it
'Cause I think I've lost my mind.
The neon sign keeps flashing
And the traffic holds its steady f low,
While I walk with you
And you are at my side.

- Bruce Rout
November 1969/ Calgary...

Drowning in Lake Superior Farther West of Wawa

I sat by the river and cried.
A hazy mountain sunset
And the river washed my eyes
In a mist of blue and yellow.

I looked an myself and said,
You're sick --
Sick as a vomiting dog.

Why are you so frightened
And why do you look at me and die?
I know you've been
extinguished
By your fear of the world.

Look at your insecurity,
How much you want to sleep.
Why are you always so tired
And things go back to bad?

Let the spark I have planted
Take the darkness by the throat
And a white snuffed-out candle
Become the sun.

- Bruce Rout

On a Boat on Lake Superior

Underwater a candle cannot
ignite
Or spark become the sun.
Whatever has happened now is
Whatever we have begun.

Nowhere can the light be seen
But on the top of a hill
Decked with royal purple
Fringed with blades of green.

What you have is the gift God can give
If only you let it be
And rest the mind in comfort
And tranquility.

- Bruce Rout

Rowing to Shore

A grocery bill lies quietly
On a neatly cleaned table top.
A pair of scissors rusts
Alone in an unused drawer.
A deck of cards
Spread across the platform
Of a station the train has left
We watched him go and waved goodbye.
We ran like people reunited
To an open-topped car --
To what was still unknown
And how it rains a drizzled spectacle
And the dust is washed in the bright array of colour
That was always there …

… underneath.

- Bruce Rout

West of Lake Superior

Where is Moulton Hill
With its road-rutted snow
And where are the lanes
With their soft streetlight glow
Where I once held you?

Where are the streetlights
That lit your face in the dark?
And where is that bridge
I followed you on
Writing notes in the air?

Where are the eyes I once saw
In a face I still hold true …
They stand beside me in the wind
And keep my back from breaking when I walk.

- Bruce Rout

Back to Wawa

She came and saw the way I was
And waved.

She stopped to say goodbye
And said hi
When we meet again.

She walks on,

And so do I.

Who knows how far a man must push himself
Just to write a poem or do what he wants?

The need to love
Sprang from the lips of the earth
And saw the life
She had borne.

She gave this life to me.
It is a gift,
For it is all she can give.

This, for all who read
Is how I see her,
And how I see her,
No man will ever know.

- Bruce Rout

Dregs

When I think of the way she views life
Through mists of clouded eyes
And know what lies beneath,
I can but take my head
And bury it in the palm of my hands.

To think what could be
If only I knew how.

To learn a man must first teach
And teach himself
What lies beneath his own core
Of ashes held by burnt matchsticks
And coloured crayons.

This is my Margaret
Whose colours vanish in purple and gray,
Whose hair has turned
From love to the beaches of Normandy.

There she lies asleep
Cloaked in her body-bed
Made of cotton
-- When will she wear white silk?

She thinks of one who is gone
And still standing here.

This knight in shining armor
Has hung his lance on the mantle
And loosed his dogs for the night
To retire by a fire
Of winter-wood
And drink his wine alone.

- Bruce Rout

Redemption

Who is this woman
And her shawl
Standing
In downtown Winnipeg in the spring?

She is young
And she is old
Like a seed
That has melted in the snow.

The wind braces itself
For yet another gust
Across open fields
Scattering
Peasants off the street.

All but one remains
Tugging at her shawl
And waiting for the sun.

- Bruce Rout

Untitled

When do we stop to call
These sweet nothings our own
As castles stand on dark-lit nights
And the rainbow cries for heaven?

God and love with tinges of ecstasy
Cried but for the reason why
We stand to die
Lying in the sand

How is it that an Englishman
Said that the 500 have stood
To fight the Persian hoard
With a hardwood board of iron?

Let me tell you, we're going to make
it,
Though the yellow hoard may come over the mountains
With their teeth and armpits flashing
And eyes that blaze in the sun.

Though there is the bomb and its fiery fear
Or the threat of slavery to the hip

Though there is the aspect of broken children,
We'll make it

In the face of television cameras
And plastic baby bumpers
And overwhelming garbage disposals
We'll let it ride and make it

When the sun is shining
Rain seems silly and umbrellas die

To be put away like unused candlesticks
Or barefoot children in the sky.

When the wine bottle is finished
It is corked by the shadow of emptiness
And shelved on a wall with drops of nothingness
To hide its own secret of ecstasy

Blue and grey, white and black,
The colours flow together
On a brush sweeping wetted canvas
To become the sky.

Lights of love in tainted windows
Blow the listless breeze
To the wind never ending
Without a flash of colour

the beat, the beat, the beat –
comes and goes

Like the moods of a woman
and the steps she takes
walking down a slippery street

Of melted pavement
And snow-washed hills
Unnoticed.

The rock is washed away to sand
In trying to communicate
What the water could tell us.

A yellow bordered highway

Pounds out the message

In words of ancient Braille

Written on a leper's parchment.

if only / if / only if –
- if and only if / if it matters at
all

Let me see, let me see ... let me see;
Where does the Nile begin but in Jerusalem?
As sure as the Hudson River
Flows from the mouth of every American,
So we must sit here like the rock
Or be turned to sit another century.

Let it be in the worst of senses
'Till it demands a resolution.

Let it go and let's see
Whatever can become of a newer world.

- Bruce Rout

Michelle took three years to write on the sides of various highways throughout the country.

Michelle

A poem covering three years of hitch-
hiking back and forth across Canada in
the second half of the 1960s. Some of this
time was spent riding on trains.

The beat
of the wheels
on the tracks
formed a rhythm

which began

the cadence

of this poem.

Michelle

Michelle points you north,
And as she walks beside you
You feel her gentle flesh
Massage the souls of your feet
From the coldness and the darkness
Of the Jaws of Death.
And then you find a lake somewhere
To drink her gentle kisses from above,
And you would walk with her
If your mind could meet the beauty of the night.
If only you could follow her persuasiveness
And touch the darkness there inside.

Michelle leads you west,
She opens up the corridor of doors
Within the rooms of your mind,
She takes your hand,
And the vastness of her wonder
Keeps recurring and recurring
As the sweat between her fingers
Flows into your veins of passion
And you wish to bend down to hold her
If you could rise to meet her
And you wish that she would be yours
If only she would let you.
For you sink below your loneliness
As you walk with her by her side.

Michelle lifts your head
To meet the gentle rushing of her bosom,
And you see the whiteness of the life forgiving food
Upon the nipples of her wonder.
You know what you have found therein
Within the space of time and love
To place your head upon her breast
To hear the pounding of her love,
And wonder with amazement
Of your own astonishment
And you feel the presence of the one above the clouds.
And you wish that she could lift you
To go up and greet him,
And you wish that she could hold you
From the terror of your flight,
And pray that she will love you
When you are gone.
Michelle lets you build a cabin there,
The temple of your dreams
In the loneliness of paradise.
And she helps you with the foundations
Of the valley of her chastity
And encloses the walls with rooms of exuberance
And touches the roof of virtue
With the floor of happiness,
And leads you to build a fire there.
And you wish that you could hew the wood
And mar the beauty of her hair,
If only you could swing the axe
To scar the emptiness of time.
For now you must go back again
To face the emptiness and loneliness surrounding.
And as your head leaves her breast
To roam her splendor
Clothed always in the green of morning,
You know that you now have her

To be yours now and forever.

Samuel de Champlain,
You came with the smell of Normandy
Still fresh upon your lips;
And as you kissed the back of her knee
You left a scent which lingers on forever,
You hoped that you could warm her
In the heat of January,
And you wanted to explore her
To her shameless hidden womb
And you wanted to caress her
On the calluses of her winged feet.

Michelle tantalizes you
To touch her naked legs of beauty.
And keeps her knees of cleanliness
In your heart of frustration.
And you wish that you could sustain her
And make her understand
That you once possessed her
By the waters of the west.

Michelle holds you for the end of time
And clenches with her fingers
On the veins behind her knees,
And you feel the rush of nausea
Keep coming and surrendering
By the waters of the St. Lawrence.
You knew her as the woman you have loved
Which you shall hold in the rooms of remembrance
To recall that you once loved her
And held her to be yours.

Michelle remember,
That somewhere in St. Malo

Lies a Norman that once loved you.
For from his dying lips
Rose his words like perfume
Which walked across the sea
And knelt before you in adoration;
Keep it with you always
For it is the word of love,
Wear it in your hair
As a fleur-de-lis,
It is a part of you and will never die.

Somewhere in Newfoundland
Sits a fisher mending nets,
His hands like sand
Weave a long of legend.
Where he sits men fought and died,
Their bodies decayed into rock
Upon which sits a fisher,
Mending nets and telling stories
And listening to the wind.

Michelle takes your hand
And with your skill
Binds your heart to the rock and fog.
And with your eyes scans the sea
And sends you out to fish.
You disappear in the haze
Which is the eternity you live
And makes you lose yourself
In the depths of thought
And the darkness of a moonlit sea.

Michelle takes the hand
Of a lumberjack
And with his sceptered axe
Gleans her body painlessly,

While the flashing metal
Sings of trappers and courier-de-bois,
Of canoes and furs and heavy drinking
And of a land not yet born.

Wolfe you never saw Michelle
Sitting in the midst of prairie wheat,
Or walking tightrope horizons at dawn.
Yet she has an enchantment
You cannot understand
But only sit and meditate upon.
What very strange child is this
You have seen standing on a cliff?
Just born by her father
To be reared by her mother.
As you take her and embrace her
And try to keep her as your own.
Michelle persuades you to cherish
The love of fellow men
And thereby to establish
The seed of dreams to come,
For once you came a sailor
And like all others, a sailor you shall be
In the epoch of eternity.
There is a dream which lives today
Carried by a breath of wind
Spoken in St. Malo,
And expanding the mind of a man
Who has yet to come today.

Sir Isaac Brock,
You caught her in the agony of rape
And her chastity was defended
By the smell of a perfumed kiss
And a bandaged wound now mended.
If only she was not desired

By the muzzled hawk below,
And if only you could keep her
In the arrogance of moonlight,
And never depress her from her height and bound full
way.
Yet you wanted to secure her
In the dawn of inspiration,
In a dream of love you desired her protection
And to build a wall between them
Of union in fear of degradation.

A dream was born on a dying wind
And rested on a maple tree
To grow from a sapling into maturity,
And she brings from the land
The mind of John A.
And makes him build a railway
To bind a dream together
Like a fisher
Mending nets.

The Red River flows into
A forgotten stream.
It is the colour of men
Who came and burried their hearts
In soil and sand
To gain the admiration of a girl named Michelle.
It winds its way
Through golden fields of wheat
And sings its song of marriage
To a forbidden empty grave.
And if you listen carefully
To the words it has to say
Your tears will turn
To the colour of men
And feed their hearts with sorrow.

On quiet summer nights
I lie in bed awake
With nothing but my thoughts
To keep me company,
And as I close my eyes
I hear the rustling of a pleated dress –
And see my Michelle come and take my hand
And lead me to western water.
For I always fear to go there
As she leads me on forever,
And my mind cannot follow
The reason why and where,
For I always want to overtake
Those running behind me.
Yet she clears my eyes with tears
To see her gentle beauty,
For she is ours and we are hers
As I live in my log temple
Under the eyes of the one above.

Where is the man who will come someday
And disappear in the future of our dreams?
Where is the country we will love
Before we were born and many days after we die?
Everyone can drink a cup of water
From the stream of consciousness
But only from our hands.
Somewhere there is a man who walks the river.
He holds a cup for those whose lips
Reek with the envy of melodrama.
You and I can never taste
Unless we go to greet him
Hand in hand.

- Bruce Rout

Aug. 13, 1968

Sudbury, Jasper, Toronto, Waterloo, Edmonton, etc...

Family

This poem was written about my mother who died in a head on car collision in 1961. I was 11 at the time and shortly after took to the road.

Elegy on a Blue Rose

You're looking for a reason
When you know that there is none.
You ask why,
Well why not.
You had a life for a song.
You sang it and still you ask
Why it was ended,
Halfway through.

- Bruce Rout

November 5/68
Waterloo

This is my only published poem in the 60s. It is about my brother John who is two years older than I. John has Down's syndrome and was incarcerated and institutionalized for 45 years before we got back together. We had built a cottage, John and I, in Parry Sound before our mum died. Behind the cottage is a large tree-covered hill or escarpment by the kettle lake the cottage is built beside. On the crest of this hill is a huge rock half buried in the hill where we would play as children. I missed him while I was alone along many miles of highway.

Blockade

What is that you have in the palm of your hand,
Which you hold with such tenderness?
What is that look in your face
You have when you reach to grasp it?
And what is that glow from your eyes
You see in the darkness
Whenever you look up in your search?
For this is the rock rolled away
By hands we have not seen nor held
Nor known what is kept therein.
Hold my hand and together we will strike the rock
And see sweet water gush and turn to tears and blood
And flow up to the crest where we will climb
And look, with the world at our feet
And see what will avail us.
Why do you look in my eyes such
And why do you hold me and cry?
And why is our touch separated
By an unfelt sorrow I cannot explain?
Why are my eyes clouded
With tears drunk below
As we tried to stop and touch our dreams
To each other on the rock
That keeps us together when we are apart?
Let us hold each other and stand here for a while
And wait.   - Bruce Rout

This poem was written to my friend Bruce Miller. I hitched hiked and traveled with Bruce all over the continent. We often lost each other.

The Evening Breeze

Come and find me if you can
In the shadows of some distant street.
We were friends before time began
And drank life when it would meet us.
And now we are parted –
But I can still hear your voice
Calling for me to go and find you.

- Bruce Rout

November 8/ 68
Waterloo

Bruce Miller wrote this poem. It was the only poem he ever wrote.

 i cry for the feelings of yesterday
that i should still be feeling now
i am not old enough to feel my youth escaping
my youth came late
it could not have ended so quickly
now is the time that i should be using people
for their own benefit
i should be back on the road not having money
to worry about
i should be penniless for a time being
when i can get as rich as any
unhappy unbum
whenever i want
i can only be poor now
when i can't afford it
my emotions cry
for an unemotional relationship of love
i cry

edmonton alta 21-7-69 bruce miller

I wrote this poem for my Dad. We tried to get along but it never happened. Dad was a high school teacher who won many awards for his teaching. He enjoyed the classics and, I guess, I got some of his love for Truth and honour from him. It is very difficult to portray the feelings of loss and frustration.

Insanity

What I have lost in battle
I cannot stop to count.
I know now I stand
With the sun at my back
Facing the wind
With my armour spread
About me on the ground
Shredded like paper mâché.
My sword dangles broken
From a hilt of hand-carved gold
And my shield is battered
Beyond recognition.
Nothing but the mat
Of my hair reminds
Me of a helmet
Handed me by my father
Before the battle began.
It is barely begun.
For while I call
Upon my allies
And secret weapons to mount,
There is dust on the horizon
Telling me of the coming
Of the enemies' hideous self.
For he believes I am weakest now
Standing broken on a hill of sand.
Little does he know
That in my last
Spartan victory at Thermopylae
That I have found a lance
I thought my weakness
Which cannot break
Until it is taken once again
By the father who gave it to me.

- Bruce Rout
December 19, 1970

Mood

Poetry of moods
described in the 60s

By Bruce Rout

Contrary to popular belief, there were not that many drugs in the sixties. There are a heck of a lot more drugs these days along with a modern social acceptance and promotion of their recreational use. In spite of what you may think, none of these poems, or any poems I have written, were done so under the influence of drugs. Most were written very late at night after drinking far too much coffee. One poem was written while drunk. This is not that poem. This is an important poem about a major philosophical discovery.

Pedestal

With grass growing by the road
And farmhouses on the hill,
The mist sort of takes you
And twists you all about;
The trees are maple green
And the carpet dirty gold,
The cloud is a ceiling you can touch as you walk there.
It's hidden by a roof of foliage
From the rain, which can't find you,
Or clean your clothes of sawdust.
The grass is not so green now –
But it still has a voice which can only wail or moan
When you walk on it.

---- (5 in morning, Dec. 1/ 1968)

Everything I say or write has been said before.
If you don't believe me -- don't.

(little after 5 a.m. dec. 1 etc.)

Last night I found the Universal Truth:
Got up and wrote it down.
I can't read my own writing:
And I forgot what it was.

(quite a bit after 5 am ...

Sometimes I get inspired.

Dirty Fingernails

This prison we are in
Is the forehead of the
Dreams we haven't seen yet.
This dawn we see
Is the hill of stone
We haven't climbed yet.
This day
This moment,
This now
We touch by seeing
Candles in self destruction
Is the emptiness
We see in prison
And live as we climb the hill
And touch the rising sun.

- Bruce Rout

(4 in morning, Dec. 1/ 68) Wtloo

Sometimes, like now, there is a blank page and I simply cannot bring myself to write about it. At those times, I just leave it alone. Let it be.

The Death of Another

And they burnt the effigy of morning
In the twilight of December
By the everlasting metal shining bright.
The warming of the air and its melodies delight
The design of the lonely mind.
The snow was white beneath the ashes of grief
As the second was shot in the dawn of remittance.
A nation stands and waits like a bull moose in heat
For the glow of ashes to die in inspiration and defeat.
We wait for the shadow of the olive branch
To keep the fire from extinguishing
The reasons of existence and the logic of our simple
minds.

- Bruce Rout

(day after Sen. Kennedy was shot)

A doodle.

Mental Scribblings

There's a spot of nothing in your tea,
Crowded out by the concepts of a genius.
I know it keeps reminding you of me –
and the con   ception that lies between us.

A blank page – no, really, it's really blank. Honest.

November 11/ 1968.

We still hear your marching feet on wet pavement or
loose gravel
Before you left to die in a distant land.
We still hear the noise of tanks,
Of bombs and guns firing
From places that are legend now –
Tobruk, Dieppe, Ypres, and Passchendaele.
Johnny Canuck who came as cannon fodder
And went as the victor,
Knowing your task was to be unrewarded and few there
would be
Who would still hear your marching feet
When you last left us.

- Bruce Rout

November 8/ 68
Waterloo

A poem of frustration in the middle of a stupid war and a society that eats its young.

Poem of Religious Allegory

Everywhere there are signs of things to follow.
The melting grass burns with flagrant folly
And fills my mind with thoughts of spring.

There is a brook somewhere which dies when the snow
is gone
Rushing in mad torrents throughout the year.
It brings the fresh smell of nausea
That everything lives by dying.

There is a tree somewhere which kills the sound
Of singing birds by its deafening silence.

Who walks the floor of time on his hands and kneels?

Someone kicked him in the face
And he helped him to his feet.

Tell me --
What beast roams the earth
Knee deep in the blood of its mother's womb?

Where can I find it and what must I do
To drive it into the jungles of eternity?

For it will come again and I must learn to Master it,
And there are signs of things to follow.

- Bruce Rout

Space program. I became a scientist.

Message from Mars

There goes the lady clad in white.
A dove sits upon her hand
Silhouetted against a scarlet sunset.
She is calling to us –
She is calling for us
To go and follow her footsteps which disappear into the
dark night.

- Bruce Rout

Jan. 11, 69, 3 am.

Another favorite of mine.

Talon

Strange and mixed emotions
Fill this empty cavern with eternity.
Emotional hangups and tired bodies
March in row after row.
Row after never-ending row
They come.
The sheep to the slaughter
Whose shepherd is a lamb.
Dark and dreary rooms
Lit by flashing lights of blue and red --

Welcome to California!

Land of dreams,
And open a new way of life
For the migrant nomad,
The mislead,
The discouraged broken dreamer,
The stupid ass who takes his gun
And follows Napoleon wherever he goes.

Bob Dylan is buried
Under sheets of Country music.
We can only understand
His prophesy of today.
Now his words are lost
And seem unreal
While we wait for the mystic tramp
And his iron clad deal.

- Bruce Rout & ¾ San Francisco

I was in the middle of the countryside and walked into a small, empty church to say some prayers. As I was leaving, I noticed a list of names under the heading:

"Those who Gave the Ultimate Sacrifice."

Standard

A book is written on a church wall
Rhyming the names of men with time
Who saved their lives
In broken piggy banks
And poured them out like concrete
To be the foundation
On which we walk.

- Bruce Rout

I learned to sail on Lake Ontario.

The Westwind Gap

Looking up and looking back
At the times that were before
The cloudy memory-dream clears
And the chess game chaos
Makes its move to mate.

The fisher father figure,
Net and oar in hand,
Takes his son to sea
The shape and lay of the land.

He walks away on water
And disappears behind the cloud
While his son takes the tiller
And sails on to destiny.

- Bruce Rout

Tro'n'u 26/10/69

This poem scares me. I wrote it to Roger White, a wonderful Canadian poet, who wrote <u>Witness of Pebbles</u>. This poem is in response to his poem, "The Pioneer." The thing that scares me is that this poem was written about twenty years before Roger wrote his. Freaky, eh?

Dangerous Street Corners

What is new? What is old?
What is young will die.

What knowledge of eternal truth
Do you carry in your shoes?
What have I learned and forgot?
What have I forgotten to learn?
There may be nothing
Behind the silver screen of paradise,
For my mind is empty
From the religious experience –
And can never be filled
Or drained.

BR Toronto 26/10/69

Caffeine

coffee coffee coffee –
Takes your mind for you
Wraps it around your finger ands ties it into a neat little
bow.
Coffee is the colour of midnight,
Its perking is the sound of a clock striking twelve...

Ah the fantasy of India
Whose black cobra stands knocking
At the door of some Pakistani monk.

- Bruce Rout

If you close your eyes you can plainly see that this page
is blank.

A pedantic poem. Somewhat pragmatic.

Is Peace Worth It?

It's alright man
The elephants are coming and the hill's about to break.
Our mind is expanded
Until your will is shaking.
Bombs and guns and violence
By campfire in the night
Prove again that the war is on
And the dove is flying home away from the noise and
fear.
Our love will find a way
To get to the generals,
The bleeding footsore soldier,
And the empty caverns calling.
Our voice is sure; our hearts are strong
And our cause comes
From the bloodied earth
Until we're covered by the sea.

- Bruce Rout

Calgary

Sometimes I wonder if anyone cares.

No Return Address

The smell of burnt sawdust
In the air of a hundred years leaves a memory of what
was now.
In a thousand years
May someone come
And discover this last remaining mark
Of a hand groping from the soil –
Black and charred,
Exhausted in defeat,
Died struggling to gain the impossible.
Let that someone come;
Perhaps some explorer, frightened by what has been,
Will pick it up
And appreciate it
More than we ever could.
This is our land
This is our Canada
We honour, cherish and love,
This is our life which is slowly crumbling
And dying with us.

- Bruce Rout

Edmonton

I was waiting to meet with a Rev friend of mine while he was busy working his congregation. As I waited I saw the most interesting sight.

Edmonton Sunday

Sunday morning
And the sun is shining

Time, time, time, time, time,

A pendulum walks
Carrying
a fishing rod over his shoulder
Followed by a line of hungry cats.

A white walled church
Empties to the sound
Of birds singing.

Cars start
And a lonely minister
Dressed in black
Waves goodbye
To this ominous parade.

- Bruce Rout.

Touching a Pendulum while Half Blinded by Darkness

All your life I have heard you when you called me.
I've shared your moments of happiness.
I've run to and from
Caves of exterior notion
And dared to come again
When the rain no longer shines.

The bullets are lead and gone tomorrow
As the dawn fires its last return –
And the waves of freedom keep getting bigger
And evolve into an everlasting calm.

Come again and grow together.
We cannot do each the other wrong.
Open are the stairwells to adventure
And closed again are the falls and rapids.

Fools go on with their pretending
But we've managed pretty well on our own.
A computer-minded ashtray
Blows everything asunder
And reigns as the victor once again.

Pens flourish in a sea of roller bearings
As motor cycles chase away the sun.

We're going back to Québec City
And find again the life we had before.

We're no longer here as finite wanderings
For the clouds have up and disappeared,
The rainbows shine as Truth rearranging
And your heart is sown together.

- Bruce Rout

My son tells me that he is tired of hearing poems about sex. There are a lot of poems about sex. It isn't done all that well -- or at least that's what our women tell us. So I wrote this poem long, long before he was born. It's about sex. And no, am not gay. I am not a druggie, sex pervert, or in any way perverse. I am normal ...

Quont

(wherefore and why?)
We come and go into strange and wonderful
Light bulbs and cease to excrete the strange mentality
Of our bodies.

Listen to the sound of the birds...
My life expands something like the air of a concrete
balloon.
Have you ever noticed how small your head feels
When you hold it
Between your two fingers ?
Bruce is just horny
But I just die
Rain is the form of forgiveness.
Perhaps if I walk in the rain
I will become sober.
It is a horrible thing to die
From alcoholic poisoning.

 hrelp?
Cough ---- sneeze
Sneeze ----death
Death ----- love
Love ---- death
Death ---- cough cough.
What?

- Bruce Rout.

This poem is self explanatory.

Unknown Soliloquy

The black knight
Is running from
A monstrous shadow
Known as God.
His armour pierced
By thunder bolts of love –

Everyone is going mad.

Dogs dig in beaches
To bury their heads,
Chains are worn
About their necks and grass grows from their eyes.

Cars go backwards
Down a one-way alley
And scratch their hoods with their glasses.

Pills come in colours of red and blue,
The bottle is paved in white,
And the tongue of
A prophet's warning
Is perched on the top of the Black Knight's lance.

- Bruce Rout

Ah, a peace poem, I think.

Elephantasie

It's hard to write freedom
When it's seen that way;
When the echo chamber sings love
And the horizon is the earth's apron string.
Freedom's song is stretched across your eyes
Like a single line of music
And speaks one
Word of friendship and welcome.

Then slips away from sight
Waiting for your
Arrival on a bed of ivory.

- Bruce Rout

San Francisco.

I recommend reading Leonard Cohen's treatise on the poet who cannot sleep. Then again, the CBC did a black and white piece about Cohen. He talks about not sleeping in it. He visits these great 24 hour coffee shops on St. Catherine's at odd hours. I don't know what he does during even hours.

Mousetrap

(I Refuse to Sleep)

So once again I came down
To the river of the city
And wept salt tears
Until the river was dry.

My questions are run out
And my body is tired from heaving.

The answers flow one in the other
And pass before me
With one continuous stream –
And the mass forbearance
Makes me sleep
In the image of insomnia.

- Bruce Rout
San Francisco...¢

A poem for cold winter nights by the fire.

Day at the Beach

Seeds sown on faraway hills
Fed by the sun's caress,

Sails flowing like dragon flies
On wind-whipped seas of tranquility,

Leaves rustling –
Children,

Overflowing stars,
Sit on a seven string guitar
And speak words of music
So your ear's melody
Has the air of enchantment.

- Bruce Rout

A poem about not being able to write a poem.

Block

There are times
When I feel like dying,
When the night's mystic air
Of inspiration means nothing.

When walking alone
Brings not the security
Of loneliness.

When sitting
At a coffee tablecloth
With no lines of poetry running through me,

When I feel the whole world
Might just as well be at an end.

Sometimes.

- Bruce Rout

Calgary Nov.9 /69

Ah, a Christmas poem!

Is Joseph OK?

All in all
This empty bottle wineglass
Takes the shape of life and tranquility.

There is the way of time captured in the sand –
The sea of coffee grains riding on the surf
Carries the ecstasy of mermaids
On the backs of giant whales ...

Go on,
and on,
and on …

Through the confines of Ecclesiastes
And see if wind and sand will hold together
The foundation we all seek.

There is no other way –
There and here with all its misfortunes
On a backless bed of seaweed
And gossip half truth lies
And all that makes society what it is.

It may be small but it's all we got.
Then again you could sleep in the stable –
That flashing neon sign outside the
Window didn't used to work.

Funny how these things happen in the night.

Had some weirdo on a camel
Asking for your names
When he knew them all the time.

Time, Time, Time –

There is no other way to put it.

The straw may bother you
But a blanket can help a lot
Especially when it's all you got.

So don't cry sweet Mary –
I got the feeling it's going to be all right.

A stable,
a stable,
two pence for a stable.

Who will buy.
Who Will buy?

Canter, canter 'round the open air.
Horses descending on the golden stair,
Saddles of gold and hair that's white.
Won't you go for a ride tonight?

What?

The rider comes to taunt me again
With his ivory little game of chess?

- Bruce Rout, Calgary, dec 2 69

Another poem about not being able to write a
poem.

More Block

Oh God I want to write,
I want to take this pen
And hold it
And play
With numbers
Or little word games
Or draw the beating frustration
Of a nation
Into language.

BR

A true story.

Graffiti

I have returned
From an incense-scented washroom
And I have heard
The strange words it had to tell me.

There was no dime slot
For me to crawl under
And no remains
Of empty cigarette butts.

Nothing but opening straight onto the street
And the taped music player of a beating rhythm
Of people.

- Bruce Rout

Calgary, November 22/69

A barren bomb bleak land
They came to call Vietnam.

On this land they stand
And know that here poppies cannot grow
And we cannot remember them.

- Bruce Rout
November 17 69
Calgary

An antidisestablishmentarianistic poem.

OK

It's the weekly, yearly meeting of the local PTA.
Johnny's grown his hair long
And Mary's been sent away.
Mrs. Agatha is all up tight
'cause she missed her little pill today
And I think she's a little late.
Bob Thornton's a little on the woozy side
Nursing that head of his.
He wouldn't be here but for Junior's conviction
And Momma's fear of society.

What's to be done?
What's to be done?
With the youth -- our children
And the rights we all enjoy?

I think they're wrong.
They're all too young
To appreciate what we've done for them.

Let us all go, then
To bury our heads in the sand
And hide from the dark lights shining
On the wall of prosperity.

- Bruce Rout

Calgary, winter '68.

My Room

Frost is sitting like some unclassified bird upon my
mourning window.

I must leave some bread crumbs in case it thinks I have
no fear
Of ingratitude or inhospitality.

Looking down on the road below I see the cars begin to
belch
And whimper when they wake.

Pedestrians crossing on the
Window of my room,
Heads buried in blanket collars.

I had to sleep by the stove last night
Using the floor as a pillow.
It was cold, not from the air,
But from the attitude of cold blankets.

I'm too accustomed to your being there.

Times of walking
In and out of the great railroad waiting room
Come and go

Just like the weather,
the rain,
and the snow.

The wind howls
and death
Walks behind,
Invisible as a cat

Or an unmarked police car.

This is my lonely room.

I stand naked beneath the sun facing December
With wild notions
Of going home.

The great audacity
Of life
Is this room
Braced up by four
Joining walls.

In the middle is this ridiculous sleeping bag, tested at
48 degrees.

My God, my God,
Where has my woman gone?
Damascus, Athens, Rome … eternity.
She has gone where no man has been
And where no man can go

Love,
 love,
love …

She forgot to take her bible
For there it lies
In the middle of a sleeping bag
Holding four walls at bay.

Out the window runs the river
Of dust and forgotten cigarette butts.

Mormon came, and Mormon has gone.

He will not come again
But life goes on
In its terror of darkness and gloom.

And the audacity of it all
Is this hideous room.

- Bruce Rout
November 15 1969, Calgary

Finally, a poem about being able to write a
poem.

Unblock

No, no, my pen will not keep still
While it moves between the white lines
Of a one-way intersection.

This quill, this feather,
This ballpoint pen excretion,
This implement of writing
Which walks at odd hours
From streetlight to streetlight
Will sing its one time stanzas
Upon the concrete parchment
To the beat of footsteps,
Of lovers,
 and horseless statues.

- Bruce Rout
Calgary Nov./69

I read the bible all the way through a couple
of times. Once when I was 16 and again when
I was 18. Good book.

Elijah 2

There is no way to turn the day into night
They say, but I say
The world will be as black as coal
When man is through working on an earth as round as
ours.

There's no way to delay
That trouble coming every day.
There's no way to delay
The black-burning plague
That hoards its deathly path
On every highway

The oceans,
the oceans,
Aren't fit for man or beast.

What has happened to the source
Of Jeremiah and the cave of Elijah?

A small quiet voice
Follows the thunder and lightning.

It makes us to go fearlessly
To meet the daemon-dragon
That threatens us so.

-Bruce Rout
Calgary Herald
March 6/ 1970

Ignore the sixties. They didn't happen. Apparently if you remember anything about the sixties there is something wrong with you. The sixties are over. They have absolutely no significance or bearing on today whatsoever. They are just an historical curiosity. Imagine, an entire generation of kids who are running around saying that through the acquisition and dissemination of a particular knowledge we can establish an everlasting world peace and justice for all. Obviously these people are out of their minds. Pay them no attention. As we all know, humanity can only be saved through a strong economy. If you want to help mankind, talk to your bank manager or human resource officer. They know what they are doing.

Shit

A collection
of meaningless
'60s poetry

by Bruce Rout

Pandora

Short dresses, long skirts,
Hair spread out on a pillow;

Quick little glances
Into completely different worlds;

The flick of a tongue
Upon the upper lip,

The little finger
Held daintily aloof

Short curls leading to cheeks
That should be wet with tears.

An empty volume was written to them
From the beginning to the end –

How to love and despise
Their uptight -- exasperating ways.

- Bruce Rout

Tr a awn a 26/10/69

Cufflinks

I don't want to fall in love with you
Though I've searched for you 'till the end of the sea
And seen your face on painted rain drops
From endless clouds.

I don't want to hold your hand or let you take my hand
in yours
As we walk arm in arm
Through the dusty cobwebs of streetlights.

I don't want to be with you
Just when we're together,

And I don't want to be alone
When we are apart.

Just let me walk and look for you
In sunshine valleys,
And maybe I'll see you on rainbows as I stroll
From sea to sea.

Edmonton

Alberta
- Bruce Rout

In the late sixties and early seventies, there were hundreds of very young women – 17, 18, early 20s, wearing skimpy mini skirts, bare legs with knee-high boots and furry vests and it's 35 below zero. They froze. They paced, often alone, often with boyfriends and pimps, strutting the sidewalk with impunity among the many cops, taxi cabs and Johns. Seventh Avenue in front of the York Hotel and Legion in Calgary was famous for them. Sometimes there would be the odd hanger-on at three and four in the morning in the deathly cold night. Words fail me.

To all Whores Everywhere

Red Roses surround the walls
Of prairie Jordan in the east.

The wind whips cold and harsh
Through the streets of Winnipeg
Like a woman running in fear
From the ice and snow
Of last winter.

A cold water flat
Is nothing more
Than a feeling
Deep inside
That wells up
And hides itself sometimes in tears.

The many tavern entrances
Decked by the beauties of the town
Are cedar-down
And filled with doves.

When you see
Bruce again
Say hi
And that I will return
To haunt his dreams.

What little we
All know of evil.

There is a space between your ears
Made of gypsy-rum
That runs like a river
As it sloshes back and forth.

We roll from one end of the country
To the other
In an Apocalyptic search of time which marches on.

Now that angels
Rest their feet
In a hot bath
Of chocolate and honey
Made by the hands
Of a gypsy band,
Can the hand
That rules the world
Bowl nine-pins on a Saturday?

Now that ships are locked
Out to sea
Sand and shore are one.

Can the man
Stop for a moment
To think of time
In a universal nut-shell?

Can the man
Think for himself?

Can the man
Decide
What is right or wrong?

Can the man
Be silent
Just a second
And say what is on his mind?

The gypsy-bandwagon
Has come to town
And cedar-wooded mountains
Fall down like goose and geese
And downy-feathers
All decked out
In the riding leathers.

Write a letter to dad.
Say you're glad.
Don't be bad.
'Cause it's sad
You're going away so soon.

- Bruce Rout

The wise women of Vancouver.

Cow on the Moon

There are people on the streets of Vancouver
Clothed in red and green
Looking at shop windows.

There are harbour moons on the roof-tops of the city
That shine incessantly throughout the day.

There is a spirit clad in white cotton
Carrying a candle like a wisp of wind
Along the beach.

She sees and smiles
At all of us
Like a mother hen
Sailing on a boat of seaweed
On a shore of grass.

- Bruce Rout

Ah, this one. Let's see, I'm in Vancouver trying to write. But it is so late that the sun is about to come up and I won't be able to be creative. My window faces east towards what will soon be the rising sun. There is a tree outside blocking the view of the onset of sunrise.

Knocking on Wood

Things that make me sad are the things I must write
Before the dawn steals through my window
Taking away my lines of extravagance.
Things are sad when the nothingness
And silence of death creeps through the mind.

What we are looking for is an array of colour.
The only problem is our world is black and white.

Life is the constant step of pictures
In a darkly-lit hallway
Covered by the veil of black frames we call windows
Through which steal lines of poetry
Shading the dawn beneath a tree.

Maples and oaks have stood the test of time long
enough
To keep us standing beneath the rain.

Everyone who can sing, can live
A life of dancing.

The sun shines hanging from a golden cord
In a sea-empty blue cloud of dust
We call …

…the air.

Damn.

What hideous things are hidden deep within a woman's
mind
Concerning her man that drives him mad
And makes him rue the day he was ever born?

There is a limit to communication!
And the question answer period caught between two
commas.

Thirteen different people
Change their sex from day to day
Without even seeing the doctor
That delivered them from the womb
Of a monk's fantasy

When time has stopped
Becoming from day to day
And the words of love have run dry
Like the Gobi Desert trampled by Marco Polo's camel,
When we have failed to understand the nature of
loneliness
Lying beneath a tree in Eden …

Is Adam sleeping, waiting for his rib
To be returned in the form of an apple's core
Wrapped in a two-edged sword?

When will the time come
For the rock to be struck, not too often,
For the children of Israel?

When will a woman see
That she
Is nothing more than the edifice

Of a man's sleeping body
Lying beneath a tree
In Eden?

- Bruce Rout

In our house basement, before our family fell apart, my Dad had a study where I used to hide. He was a geography teacher and had these really neat atlases and maps and stuff that I would go through for hours and hours on end.

My Father's Atlas

If the Giant's beans grow green
On a windowsill of twilight
The earth may never be the same again.

The world
The world …

 That
Upon the windowsill sits

Can never the same be,
In its new-found ecstasy
Within the Giant's womb.

The world …
        Sitting on a beach
        Is nothing but the sea
        Rolling in wave
        After wave

Singing a mermaid's melody.

Is never the world
The same unfurled
On a beach that surfs like a Giant's fur?

Is the world nothing,
Nothing but people?

Is the people the Giant
Of whom we sing and sit upon
In our dour mentality?

And is the Trans-Canada Highway

Made of sand
And sandstone?

Well, shit
Trudeau's married again
To the woman even Michelle would be of jealous of
And the things we sit and dream of
Are nothing but sand.

Is the edge of the world in Siberia
Or are the sands of time consumed
By an Amsterdam whore?

Where does the dyke end
But in orgasm?

Is there a cross purpose in the sitting of friends to
dinner
And is a steak sandwich made of clay?

Where is a lover's head
But in the sand?

The world turns
On the axis of grief
And the sun shines
Behind a cloud.

Is the end near
… or is the game we play that of eternity?

Can a car re-group
And sing the songs of yesterday
Or is it all for nothing
Like a drive
Into the deep black night?

When the jumping up and down
Has become the essence of eternity
And the Trans Canada Highway
Has become un-paved.

The women of the world
Are unraveled
Across the parchment of stone.

The world …
The world

Has stood upon its ear and never seen the light.

Never before in the history of creation
Has the sea been green before.
The trees that stand upon the windowsill
Are made of green and gold.

Their trunks are boughs
That are the Giant's toothpicks.

The world has stood on its ear
And seen the sunset that sits on the windowsill
Of the Giant's pendulum
That no man has seen.

The world …
The world

When will it begin to rise
Against the ecstasy
To me?

- Bruce Rout

Glassy Jak

A cigarette burns
Inside a dirty ashtray
While the sound of glasses
On a whisky table-top
Blurts out a music
And sets the pace of a smoke-filled bar.

Here is a lonely escape –
A recluse from the sun
Taken in an ice-chilled glass
With a background
Of mini-skirted bar-maids
And silk-covered legs.

Somewhere below the carpet
Camouflaged in red and filth
Lies a hope not yet seen
For all those who seek
A better way than the alternative.

- Bruce Rout

And so we end on a blank page. You see, this book has 160 pages, which divides by eight. Each folio has eight pages, four on each side, meaning the book must have a number of pages which is divisible by eight. Fractional pages are not allowed. So, even blank pages have purpose. Ah, they also serve who are only blank and stand in line endlessly like our great Canadian nation. May all of you be inspired to create some art, of whatever form, to let the universe, and the earth beneath our feet, know that we are here. May God bless all of you.